MINISTRY OF
ORTHODOX LITURGICAL MUSIC

In Memory of
Fr. Dimitri Ressetar
(+ 1985),

and

Dedicated to
Fr. Paul Lazor.

Ministry of
Orthodox Liturgical Music

by

David Barrett

Foreward by
Father Sergei Glagolev

Orthodox Liturgical Press
Southbury, Connecticut
January 2018

Library of Congress Cataloging-in-Publication Data
Barrett, David
1956 –
    Conducting and Rehearsing Orthodox Liturgical Music

    Library of Congress Control Number: 2016921617

MINISTRY OF
ORTHODOX LITURGICAL MUSIC

Orthodox Liturgical Press
Southbury, CT 06488

ISBN 978-0-9915905-6-8

Printed in the United States of America.

CONTENTS

FOREWARD

While it is important for choir directors to master the skills for the ministry of conducting choirs, it is equally important for all of the choir members to be aware of the various elements, musical, liturgical, and spiritual, that are necessary for their own ministry of Orthodox liturgical singing. The essential elements of the ministry of Orthodox liturgical music have been wonderfully presented by David Barrett in this valuable book.

Fr Sergei Glagolev

East Meadow, NY

October 2017

Fr Sergei Glagolev is a renowned music teacher and composer of Orthodox liturgical music.

PREFACE

This book is somewhat of a parallel to my earlier work, ***Conducting and Rehearsing Orthodox Liturgical Music***.[1] Whereas that particular opus dealt specifically with the ministry of Orthodox liturgical music for the choir director, this present work presents the elements of that ministry for the regular choir singer. As such, there are many parts of the previous book included again in this volume. Other aspects of the ministry that are uniquely shared only by choir directors have been omitted in the current work.

Once again, I thank Fr. Sergei Glagolev for his unfailing commitment to this ministry, for his feedback and corrections on the current book, and for again providing a wonderful Foreward to it.

May God grant all who embrace this ministry of Orthodox liturgical music do so with prayerful commitment, to His glory!

---

[1] Barrett, David, *Conducting and Rehearsing Orthodox Liturgical Music*, OLP (Orthodox Liturgical Press), Southbury, CT, July 2016.

1
ICONOGRAPHY OF
ORTHODOX LITURGICAL MUSIC

There are many levels of preparation that a Church singer needs to participate in before he or she can effectively function in this ministry. The major part of this book addresses the physiological, executional (singing), theoretical (music theory), directional (using the hands for beat patterns and expression), and preparatory (rehearsal) elements required to master the basic skills of Orthodox liturgical singing. However, two additional, yet essentially vital, areas for a Church singer are the need for spiritual and liturgical preparation.

A.   SPIRITUAL PREPARATION

Since liturgical singing is a *ministry*, that is, a participation in the two-natured aspect of the Church that, as the Body of Christ, is both divine and human, all Church singers must be communing Orthodox Christians who actively, consistently, and seriously participate in the life of the Church, as those who have been baptized to die and rise with Christ through living the sacramental life. This includes continuous participation in the Sacrament of Penance (Holy Confession), a regular, prayerful, and disciplined Communion in the Holy Eucharist, and participation in various other Sacraments, as called to (Holy Unction, Holy Matrimony, Holy Orders, etc.). As Leonid Ouspensky wrote in the book*, The Meaning of Icons*:

> "In order to receive and pass on the testimony [of Holy Tradition], the iconographer must not only believe that it is genuine, but must also share in the life, by which the witness of the revelation lived, must follow the same way, that is, be a member of the body of the Church. Only then can he transmit the testimony received consciously and exactly. Hence the necessity for continual participation in the sacramental life of the Church; hence also the moral demands the Church makes of iconographers. For a true iconographer, creation is the way of asceticism and prayer, that is, essentially, a monastic way. Although the beauty and content of an icon are perceived by each spectator subjectively, in accordance with his capacities, they are expressed by the iconographer objectively, through consciously surmounting his own 'I'

and subjugating it to the revealed truth – the
authority of the Tradition."[2]

This essential requirement for a serious
participation in the life of the Church and the
corresponding spiritual preparation on the part of
the iconographer is the very same participation and
preparation required of the Church musician, singer
and director alike. Both iconography and Church
singing are considered liturgical ministries, and, as
such, require the same disciplines.

These spiritual disciplines result in clarity of
mind, which is essential both in the spiritual life and
in the task of fulfilling the various ministries of the
Church. The following enumerates this clearly:
> "There are two means by which we can
> acquire such clarity of mind: the first and
> most necessary is prayer, by which we must
> implore the Holy Spirit to pour His divine light
> into our hearts. This He will surely do, if we
> truly seek God alone and sincerely strive to
> obey His will in everything, willingly submitting
> in all affairs to the advice of our experienced

---

[2] Ouspensky, Leonid and Lossky, Vladimir, *The Meaning of Icons*, trans. G.E.H. Palmer and E. Kadloubovsky, SVS (St Vladimir's Seminary) Press, Crestwood, NY, 1982, p. 42.

spiritual fathers and doing nothing without
asking them.
The second method of exercising the mind is
always to examine things and probe deep for
knowledge of them, in order to see clearly
which of them are good and which are bad.
We should judge them not as the world and
the senses do, but as they are judged by right
season and the Holy Spirit, or by the word of
the divinely-inspired Scriptures, or that of the
holy fathers and teachers of the Church. For if
this examination and deepening of knowledge
is right and proper, it will quite certainly
enable us to understand clearly that we must
with all our heart regard as valueless, vain and
false, all that the blind and depraved world
loves and seeks."[3]

Silence, solitude, and stillness are necessary
elements to "quiet" the self, in order to hear the
"still, small voice" of God in the heart (1 Kg 19:12):

[3] *Unseen Warfare, the Spiritual Combat and Path to Paradise
of Lorenzo Scupoli*, edited by Nicodemus of the Holy
Mountain and revised by Theophan the Recluse, translated by
E. Kadloubovsky and G.E.H. Palmer, introduction by H.A.
Hodges, M.A., D.Phil, Professor of Philosophy, SVS Press,
Crestwood, NY, 1978, p. 90.

"Our heart is, therefore, the shrine of the intelligence and the chief intellectual organ of the body. When, therefore, we strive to scrutinize and to amend our intelligence through rigorous watchfulness, how could we do this if we did not collect our intellect, outwardly dispersed through the senses, and bring it back within ourselves – back to the heart itself, the shrine of the thoughts? It is for this reason that St Makarios – rightly called blessed – directly after what he says above, ads: 'So it is there that we must look to see whether grace has inscribed the laws of the Spirit.' Where? In the ruling organ, in the throne of grace, where the intellect and all the thoughts of the soul reside, that is to say, in the heart. Do you see, then, how greatly necessary it is for those who have chosen a life of self-attentiveness and stillness to bring their intellect back and to enclose it within their body, and particularly within that innermost body within the body that we call the heart?"[4]

---

[4] St Gregory Palamas, "In Defense of Those who Devoutly Practice a Life of Stillness", *The Philokalia: The Complete Text, Volume IV*, compiled by St Nikodemos of the Holy Mountain and St Makarios of Corinth, translated from the

At the St Sergius Orthodox Institute in Paris in 1997, Dr Dimitri Conomos gave a lecture entitled, "Early Christian and Byzantine Music: History and Performance". In the second section, which he called "Liturgical Music and Orthodox Spirituality", Dr Conomos cited three fundamental concepts in Orthodox spirituality that can be made to apply to our Church music. These are the following (these sections are direct quotes from his lecture):

1. *Asceticism* is the call for self-denial, self-dissatisfaction; and the constant yearning for improvement through hard work and energetic application....The Church singer has a sacred profession, and this sanctity requires a determination of character, a strong faith, great modesty, and a high sense of integrity. To be a Church singer in an Orthodox Church is to respond to a calling, to a vocation – it demands purity, sureness of faith, and conviction.

Greek and edited by G.E.H. Palmer, Philip Sherrard, Kallistos Ware, with the assistance of the Holy Transfiguration Monastery (Brookline), Constantine Cavarnos, Dana Miller, Basil Osborne, and Norman Russell, Faber and Faber, London, England, 1995, p. 334.

2. **Holiness**. And what is meant by the **holiness** of our vocation?...Holiness means otherness, sacredness, apartness – not the common or the ordinary, but the unique, the particular, the uncontaminated.

3. **Apatheia, or "passionlessness"**....This idea of passionlessness is perhaps most reflected in the best Orthodox iconography – where the saint is painted in colours and shapes that transcend everything that is fleshly, sensual, and cosmetic.

These truths are so ontological that they are beginning to be recognized even in the secular world. James Jordan, in his textbook, **Evoking Sounds**, says the following:

"Access can only be gained through quiet and stillness within oneself.   Quiet solitude must be a daily occurrence. Stillness is a deliberate choice. You must consciously choose stillness. Unfortunately, the world will not give it to you. Additionally, you must choose stillness over and over again in very difficult situations when it might be easier not to choose stillness. Initially, the discovery of stillness

within oneself brings great joy. Soon,
however, it brings difficulties and darkness.
You will discover that the newfound stillness
unmakes personality so you can become a
person. By being still, you are able to make
yourself less so others can become more.
Also(,) by being still, the process of making
yourself less allows the music to speak clearly
through the ensemble."[5]

This process of "making ourselves less so
others can become more" is reminiscent of the
words of St John the Baptist (whom our Lord said
was the greatest born of woman), when he said, "He
[Christ] must increase, but I must decrease" (Jn
3:30). Through this process, we surrender our entire
selves, our egos, our preconceptions, our prejudices,
our tastes, likes, and dislikes, to God, so that
everything that we do in this ministry of Orthodox
liturgical music is for **His** glory, and **not** for ours. The
demons of individualism, selfishness, pride, and

---

[5] Jordan, James, *Evoking Sound: Fundamentals of Choral Conducting*, Second Edition, Foreword by Morten Lauridsen, with chapters by Robert W. Rumbelow and James Whitbourn, GIA Publications, Inc., Chicago, IL, 2009 (hereafter referred to as "*Evoking Sound*"), p. 18.

jealously must be rooted out, and, as our Lord has said, "This kind never comes out except by prayer and fasting!" (Mt 17:31; Mk 9:29). It is easy to become self-centered to the point of making the music an end in itself. For example, even though the Typikon specifies a certain number of stikhera for the day and the saints on "Lord, I Call Upon You," many parish priests, for the pastoral purpose of keeping the length of Vespers to a comfortable level for his parishioners, will limit the singing of stikhera for the saints to only those who are considered major saints, like, St Sergius of Radonezh. However, there those Church singers who eagerly try to talk their pastors into doing all the stikhera called for in the Typikon, even for minor saints whom nobody in the parish has heard of. Surrendering ourselves to God to serve **Him** in **His** Church ("**Your** will be done, on Earth as it is in Heaven!") ensures that things are done "decently and in order" (1 Cor 14:40) in the balanced perspective of humble service in the ministry of Orthodox liturgical music.

B.   LITURGICAL   PREPARATION

Another vital but often-overlooked area of preparation for Church singers is that of liturgical preparation. There are many directors who have great difficulty in their ministry because they do not know the order of the services beyond the Saturday evening Great Vespers and the Sunday morning Divine Liturgy. Services such as Vigil, Presanctified Liturgy, Funeral, Wedding, Compline, and the services of Holy Week and Pascha cause some directors great anxiety, confusion, and frustration. There are various service books of the Church that can be referred to in order to clarify the order of each particular service.[6] There are also books that give a general outline of the services with the specifics of how they differ in each of the various practices (Russian, Greek, Antiochian, etc.).[7]

Even more essential for every Church singer to realize is that liturgical music is ontologically (that is,

---

[6] A complete list of these service books is provided in the Bibliography at the end of this book.
[7] Cf. Barrett, David, *Liturgics for Orthodox Liturgical Singing, Volume 1* (July 2014) and *Volume 2* (January 2015), OLP (Orthodox Liturgical Press), Southbury, CT.

by its very being) just that: *liturgical*! As Mark
Bailey pointed out:

By principle, liturgy is not an element of music,
however important and even essential musicological
study may deem that element to be, but music is an
element of liturgy. In other words, worship is the
raison d'Ltre of the (C)hurch, and worship therefore
serves as the point of departure and the point of
arrival that should necessarily frame the entire
process of musical examination.[8]

This awareness and perspective is not only a
necessary prerequisite for all Church musicians
(especially choir members) but also a *primary factor*
in their ministry:

To start, the (C)hurch's liturgy or patterns of
worship are the primary subjects for examination. In
other words, liturgical musicians should seek broadly

---

[8] Bailey, Mark, "Toward a Living Tradition of Liturgical Music
in North America", *St Vladimir's Theological Quarterly*,
Volume 47, Number 2, 2003, p. 192.

and in detail to understand the liturgical structures, systems, and points of emphasis that specifically formulate and guide worship in the missionary (C)hurch, and to respond to this understanding with the appropriate musical expression of those elements. Musicians must also take into account the more general inclinations and manifestations of the gathered faithful in response to their communal unity in such a (C)hurch.[9]

     The order of the words in the descriptive title of "liturgical music" is thus important: It is the *liturgical* element or component that comes first and is *primary*, and *then* the musical element or component. That is, the musical element is secondary and *subservient* to the liturgical element, which gives the musical element its *only* reason for being. Otherwise, so-called "liturgical music" just ends up being secular music with a religious subject matter that is "performed" in services, rather than being the component that makes the *worship* in liturgy come alive.[10] Without this vitally essential realization and perspective on the part of Church

---

[9] *Ibid*, p. 196.
[10] *Ibid*, p. 193.

musicians, the Church singer will come to view the music of liturgy as an end in itself, divorced from its *sole* and ***primary function*** of giving shape to, enhancing, and manifesting the functions of the liturgical rites. Then, there will be more attention given to the choice of which musical arrangements of a hymn will be sung, based on musical taste and aesthetics rather than on how the setting appropriately reveals the function of the liturgical action the hymn is paired with. This essential component of liturgical preparation is even more lacking on the part of our liturgical musicians nowadays than the spiritual preparation is. It is *crucial* that *all* Church singers spend a ***great*** deal of time and study in acquiring an authentically Orthodox liturgical perspective, deeply internalizing the fact of the primacy of the liturgical component over the musical one, and examining and evaluating all musical elements, choices, and decisions in deference to the liturgical elements and their functions within the services themselves.

2
ICONOGRAPHY OF
ORTHODOX LITURGICAL MUSIC

There are many elements that Orthodox liturgical music has in common with Orthodox iconography. Both are art forms that find their expression within our Orthodox liturgical tradition.[11]

A.   MUSIC AS ICONOGRAPHY IN TIME

Orthodox liturgical music can be considered as being iconography in time. Unlike iconography itself, which, once an icon has been written, continuously exists and can always be seen and venerated, liturgical music includes a temporal co-efficient. It begins at a certain moment and ends at another certain moment. For example, a local parish may celebrate the Sunday morning Divine Liturgy beginning at 9 o'clock. It may then conclude around 10:30 that morning. During that ninety-minute period, the hymns of the service are heard, as are

---

[11] Most of the material in this chapter is based on and taken from class lectures given by Fr Sergei Glagolev at St Vladimir's Orthodox Theological Seminary, in the Liturgical Music class, "Interpretation of Liturgical Music," given in the early 1980's.

the petitions, prayers, and Scriptural readings of the Liturgy. Afterwards, at the coffee hour, the singing and hearing of these hymns can be remembered and recalled by the faithful, ***but they cannot be heard at this point because the temporal conclusion of the service is in the past!*** Therefore, the "existence" or, rather, the ***experiencing*** of the liturgical music is ***not*** a continuous one, but is celebrated within the confines of time periods.

Liturgical music, then, is analogous to iconography in that it is "painting" in time and space. It is a "verbal painting" that is ***voiced***, having a melodic line, in the worship of God. The ***function*** of music here, then, is one of ***worship***. Thus, it is something that should not be "added to" in order to make it "pretty." The beauty of the music itself stands on its own. Time and space are common denominators between liturgical music and iconography. In other words, liturgical music has iconographic forms. We "see" music acoustically with our ears (as is evident in the reference to "tone ***colors*** in the melody). Therefore, liturgy, iconography, and music are elements of worship, ***not*** of "art" per se.

The only way to ***sanctify time*** is to ***use*** it, to actually fill it up with worship (especially in the form of singing) and prayer. Timbre, that is, texture and tone color, is the "pigment" of music. Liturgical music, then, is an ***oral icon***. There needs to be a balance and a parallelism between the music and the text. The musical lines give depth and perspective to the musical "picture."

There are four aspects of liturgical music: melody, harmony, rhythm, and text. The ***text*** is the ***primary element*** of liturgical music. It is comprised of words as groupings, organized into thought units and sequences.

There are three iconographic elements of liturgical music: acoustic, evocative, and structural. The acoustic element is what is heard, how we "see" by sound. The evocative element means that the music has to be sounded, that is needs to be produced and voiced. The structural element consists of the sequential ordering of the patterns and the sounds themselves.

In the art forms of painting (iconography) and architecture (churches and chapels), the experience is observable in space and is meant to transcend space. In liturgical music (hymnography), the experience is ***observable in time*** and is meant to ***transcend time***. There is a balance of "movement" concerning liturgical music: It moves forward in physical time, but backward in the time of Church history and Holy Tradition. Liturgical music, then, is iconographic as **verbal** "imagery" in that it conveys a meaning.

Within both art forms of iconography and liturgical music, there is, as it were, a 4th "dimension" to both ministries. In iconography, we are, so to speak, looking from the inside out as a part of the experience. The observer, therefore, is a participant in that the icon, through various means such as inverse perspective, calls him into the experience of the icon. In liturgical music, we are again looking from the inside out as part of the experience. The observer is a participant in that the music, by "energizing" and ***giving life*** to the text, calls us into the reality that the text of the hymn is expressing. It makes all those who are present participants of the worship and, therefore, priests who offer the worship to God (each of us, by virtue of our Baptism and Chrismation, is a member of the "royal priesthood" of the Church [1 Peter 2:9]).

The ministry of liturgical music is the same as that of our Lord, Jesus Christ: to teach, to preach, and to heal (Matthew 4:23). The final interpretation of liturgical music we have to do ourselves via understanding the function and the content of the various hymns. The authenticity, the historical function of the hymns, should be restored. To do that, we need to make an effort to apply the interpretation of the hymnography appropriately. The only way to do that is by proper spiritual preparation, as elucidated in the previous chapter.

B. ESSENTIAL QUALITIES OF TEXT AND CHANT METER

It is important to understand the text in order to worship along with the liturgical music. Worship and prayer are heightened speech forms, called "singing." All of our hymnology (as well as the rest of the content of our liturgical services) is based on Scriptural text. Scriptural text is musical and melodic in form (prose), and should follow a free-flowing chant form. Holy Scripture, it can be said, is the "Great Lyric," used as a cantillation of salvation history. It is meant to be melodic, having cadences. It is the Truth sung in the passion of the soul. ***The text* *itself is* *melody*!**

There are some theoretical liturgical "straight-jackets." They consist of those musical devices that inhibit the understanding and the interpretation of the text. An example of this is putting the Scriptural prose into a musical context of a fixed, regular meter. This was seen by such Church fathers as St Ambrose and St Jerome, who criticized the verbal lyricizing of the Hellenists, who made the mistake of understanding the Septuagint as poetry in a regular, fixed meter. The truth of the matter is that there is a definite flow of Scriptural melodies existing in a succession of rhythmic, ***textual* accents!** ***This*** is why our music is *a*metrical, having **not** a system of fixed meters and bar lines, but rather what may be termed a ***chant* meter**, that is, combinations of various meters based on *the **accentuations** of the* **text** *itself!*

     There are some basic, essential "rules" regarding liturgical music. Free verse can **never** be inhibited by artificial restraints of fixed meter and rhyme. Free verse, using what we have called here "chant meter," divides the word groupings by **content** and ***text* accentuation**. For example, in the standard doxology, "Glory to the Father, and to the Son, and to the Holy Spirit," we may show the text accentuation as follows: "***Glo*ry to the *Fa*ther, and to the *Son*, and to the *Ho*ly *Spir*it." There are four rhythmic "pulses" from "Glo" to "Fa." Therefore, theoretically, there would be a meter based on 4 on the syllable "Glo." From "Fa" to "Son," there are five pulses, so a meter based on 5 (in this case, 2 + 3) would fall on "Fa." From "Son" to "Ho," there are again four pulses, so a meter based on 4 would fall on "Son." From "Ho" to "Spir," there are two pulses, so a meter based on 2 would fall on "Ho," as well as on "Spir." ***This*** combination of meters, in the free verse form of chant meter, would then properly accentuate the text in this example.

This use of chant meter is what is most commonly used (or, what ***should*** be what is most commonly used) in our Orthodox liturgical hymnology.

3
MUSICAL   TRAINING

In order to be an effective Church singer, a person needs to master the basic musical skills necessary to work out this ministry to the glory of God.

A.   MUSIC READING

The first skill that obviously needs to be mastered is the ability to read music. It may sound pedantic to mention that here. However, we must keep in mind that many, if not most, of our Church singers in our parishes can**not** read music. Rather, they learn the various hymns by rote, repeating them during the scheduled choir rehearsals. Many times, classes are held for free or for a nominal fee as evening courses provided at a local school in the town where this person lives. Also, there are many textbooks and tools that can assist in learning the art of music reading.[12]

B.   MUSIC THEORY

Along with basic music reading skills, the choir member also needs to master the elementary rudiments of music theory. The various building blocks of music: major and minor scales; triads and chords; 7th chords; keys and key signatures; inversions of chords; all of these must be mastered and become familiar to the Church musician. Some of our hymns are sung in sections, with dialogue with the clergy in the form of prayers. One such example is the Anaphora at the Divine Liturgy. The various sections of this hymn may begin on different notes and different chords, depending on the composition or arrangement selected. Such lack of musical skill results in longer time needed during

---

[12] Cf., for example, my *Elementary Music Theory for Orthodox Liturgical Singing*, OLP (Orthodox Liturgical Press), Southbury, CT, January 2015 (hereafter referred to as *"Elementary"*). In this textbook, I present the basic rudiments of music reading via examples taken from our Orthodox hymnology.
Therefore, the potential choir singer, while learning to read music, is simultaneously learning the hymnology itself.

rehearsals to master the music and, if the music is not totally mastered, confusion with the music (and, therefore, the singing) during the service, violating St Paul's admonition that everything in the services be done "decently and in order" (1 Corinthians 14:40).

4
LITURGICAL AWARENESS AND
MUSICAL AWARENESS

Before articulating the specifics of how to rehearse the various hymns for the services, it is important to become conscious of two elements that will make the time of the rehearsal more efficient and more meaningful. These two elements are liturgical awareness and musical awareness. Although each of these elements is a subtle one, the awareness of each will enable you to sing in a manner that is prayerful and appropriate to the liturgical services.

A.   LITURGICAL AWARENESS

Liturgical awareness refers to the function that a hymn has within a liturgical service, a feast, or an overall liturgical season. It therefore behooves the choir singers to become familiar with the liturgical theology of the Orthodox Church, and there are numerous books that cover this in detail.[13]

---

[13] Of particular importance and assistance are the works of Fr Alexander Schmemann. Cf., for example, his *For the Life of the World: Sacraments and Orthodoxy* (reprinted 2001), *Of Water and the Spirit: A Liturgical Study of Baptism* (1974),

Acquisition of this knowledge will enable the singers to interpret the musical element of the hymns in the appropriate liturgical perspective, and also allow them to sing this hymnology in a manner that reflects the reality of the particular service, feast, or liturgical season.

For example, a hymn sung during the preparatory weeks of Great Lent and throughout that season is "Open to Me the Doors of Repentance" (although called for at the Resurrectional Matins service, it is often sung in many parishes during Resurrectional Vespers where the Matins service is not celebrated). The text of this hymn is as follows:

Example 1

**Glory to the Father, and to the Son, and to the
    Holy Spirit!
Open to me the doors of repentance,
    O Life – Giver,
for my spirit rises early to pray towards
    Your holy temple,**

Great Lent: Journey to Pascha (revised edition 1974), and *The Eucharist: Sacrament of the Kingdom* (1987), all SVS (St Vladimir's Seminary) Press, Crestwood, NY.

bearing the temple of my body all defiled!
But, in Your compassion, purify me by the
    loving – kindness of Your mercy!

Now and ever and unto ages of ages! Amen.
Lead me on the paths of salvation,
    O Mother of God,
for I have profaned my soul with shameful sins
and have wasted my life in laziness!
But, by your intercessions, deliver me from
    all impurity!

Have mercy on me, O God, according to
    Your great mercy,
and, according to the multitude of
    Your compassions,
blot out my transgressions!

When I think of the many evil things I have done,
wretch that I am,
I tremble at the fearful Day of Judgment!
But, trusting in Your loving – kindness,
like David, I cry to You:
"Have mercy on me, O God!
Have mercy on me, O God!

**Have mercy on me, O God, according to
    Your great mercy!"**

Examining the text of this hymn, even without the music, it is apparent that the content of it is an acknowledgement of one's sinful inclinations and actions, and a desperate cry for help to God for repentance, healing, and salvation. This is a central theme of the entire season of Great Lent, especially the first half (the first three weeks).[14] Therefore, this hymn is **not** sung in a robust, festal manner, but somewhat slowly (without dragging!), softly, and penitentially.

In contrast to this, the troparion of Pascha proclaims the central reality of our Orthodox Faith:

Example 2

**Christ is Risen from the dead,
trampling down death by death,
and, upon those in the tombs, bestowing life!**

---

[14] Cf. Schmemann, Alexander, *Great Lent*, op. cit., pp. 76-77.

Here, the content of the hymn is one of an absolute, final victory by God over the power of alienation, sin, and death. Therefore, this hymn is to be sung in the most joyous, victorious, and celebratory manner possible.

There are hymns that combine different elements within them and, so-to-speak, shift gears, perspective, or emphasis within them. Take, for example, the troparion for Palm Sunday:

Example 3

By raising Lazarus from the dead before
      Your Passion,
You confirmed the universal resurrection,
      O Christ God!
Like the children with the palms of victory,
we cry out to You, O Vanquisher of death:
"Hosanna in the highest!
Blessed is He Who comes in the Name of the Lord!"

This hymn, reflecting the events of Palm Sunday as recorded in the Gospels, illustrates the fact that the children (as well as the adults in the Gospel accounts) cried out and shouted victoriously

the content of the last two lines of the hymn
("Hosanna in the highest! Blessed is He Who comes
in the Name of the Lord!"). Therefore, an
appropriate way to sing this hymn liturgically is to
sing the first four lines (through "O Vanquisher of
death") is a somewhat-soft-to-medium volume, and
then, to manifest the acknowledgement of Christ as
the Victorious One of God, to sing the last two lines
("Hosanna in the highest! Blessed is He Who comes
in the Name of the Lord!") in a louder volume
(without screaming) and in a robust, joyful, and
celebratory manner. This is also the case with the
second troparion for Palm Sunday:

Example 4

When we were buried with You in
**   Baptism, O Christ God,**
we were made worthy of eternal life by
**   Your Resurrection!**
Now, we praise You and sing:
"Hosanna in the highest!
Blessed is He Who comes in the Name of the Lord!"

Again, the first three lines (through "Now, we praise you and sing") are sung in a somewhat-soft-to-medium volume, and the last two lines ("Hosanna in the highest! Blessed is He Who comes in the Name of the Lord!") are sung in a louder volume (without screaming) and in a robust, joyful, and celebratory manner.

Another hymn that contains differing elements is from the Kanon of Holy Saturday (also sung at the Nocturns of Holy Saturday). Holy Saturday is a day of transition, placed between Holy Friday (the day of Christ's Passion and Crucifixion) and Holy Pascha (the day of Christ's Resurrection), the blessed Sabbath on which, as the hymns of the day proclaim, Christ experienced His own personal Sabbath by "resting" from all His works, lying dead in the tomb. The 9th ode of the Kanon clearly manifests the dual nature of this day:

Example 5

**Do not lament me,
seeing Me in the tomb;
the Son conceived in the womb without seed!
For, I shall Arise**

and be glorified with eternal glory as God!
I shall exalt all who magnify you in faith and in love!

The first three lines acknowledge the suffering of Christ's Passion and His Crucifixion on the Cross. Beginning with the fourth line, however ("For, I shall Arise), this 9th ode anticipates the victorious Resurrection of Christ from the dead that follows His Crucifixion and blessed Sabbath in the tomb. Therefore, it is most appropriate to sing the first three lines (through "the Son conceived in the womb without seed") in a very soft volume, almost reflecting the silence of the Church and all of creation as they behold Christ hanging dead on the Cross, and then, beginning with the fourth line ("For, I shall Arise"), to sing it in a much louder volume through the remainder of the ode, majestically anticipating the victory about to be wrought on Holy Pascha with Christ's Resurrection from the dead!

Many other examples could suffice to reflect the liturgical realities and perspectives of different feasts. Celebrations such as Holy Theophany (Christ's Baptism in the Jordan and the manifestation of the Holy Trinity), Holy Pentecost (the descent of the Holy Spirit onto the Church), and Dormition (the falling asleep of the Theotokos and her entrance into Heaven, anticipating the general resurrection of all of us) are just some of the feasts that make present in the Church the saving work of our loving God in His victory over sin and death and our entrance into His eternal Kingdom.

B.   MUSICAL AWARENESS

Musical awareness refers to the function of the musical elements within the hymnology of the liturgical services and their place and interaction within the various sections of the choir. Therefore, the choir singers need to be musically proficient as to how the voicings in the different parts function and how to best reflect that function in the singing of the hymnology.

A very common voice setting is found in the stikhera tones (familiar to most Orthodox as used for the stikhera on "Lord, I Call Upon You" and the Apostikha at Vespers) in the Russian Chant tradition. The following example is from tone 5:

Example 6

Lord, I call upon You! Hear me! Hear me, O Lord!

Lord, I call upon You! Hear me! Receive the voice of my

prayer when I call upon You! Hear me, O Lord!

Let my prayer arise in Your sight as incense;

and let the lifting up of my hands be an

eve - ning   sac - ri - fice!   Hear   me,   O   Lord!

Here, as with all the stikhera tones in the Russian Chant system, the *melody* is in the *alto* part. The *melody harmonization*, up parallel 3rd's from the melody, is in the *soprano* part. The *sustaining common tones* between chords are in the *tenor* part (the word "tenor" means "sustaining"). Finally, the *roots of the chords*, designating which chords are which (I, IV, V, etc.) are in the *bass* part.

What does all this mean for the choir singers? The functionality of the parts here determines which parts should be emphasized over others. Therefore, since the melody is in the alto part, the altos should be the most heard, that is, they should be the loudest part in volume, since, musically speaking, it is the most important part. Next in importance, with the melody harmonization up a 3rd, is the soprano part. This should be the next loudest part in volume. Third in importance, with the roots of the chords determining the musical harmonization, is the bass part. The basses, then, should sing more softly than the altos and sopranos.   Here, in the final place of importance with its use of the sustaining common tones, is the tenor part, which should be the softest in volume of the four parts. This does **not** mean that the bass and tenor parts should not be heard, or that the altos and sopranos should sing in an overly loud, blasting manner. It **does** mean that the choir singers should be aware of the musical function of all four parts, and adjust the volume of each part accordingly to match and manifest those functions. In fact, a good rule of thumb for **all** singers should be this: If any singer cannot hear the singers in the other three parts, that singer is singing too loudly. So, even though the altos here should sing louder than the other sections, to bring out the main melody, they still need to sing in such a manner that each alto can hear the singing of the sopranos, the tenors, and the basses. Singers in the other three sections should sing accordingly, as well.

Another common voice setting in our Orthodox hymnology is the following:

Example 7

Soprano
Alto
Tenor
Bass
As God, You a-rose from the tomb in glo-ry, rais-ing
the world with Your-self! Hu-man na - ture prais-es You as
God, for death has van-ished! Ad-am ex-ults, O Mas - ter!
Eve re - joic - es, for she is freed from bond-age and cries to You:
"You are the Giv - er of res - ur - rec - tion to all, O Christ!"

This is the Russian Chant setting for the Resurrectional Kontakion in tone 1 for the Sunday Divine Liturgy. Most of the Russian Chant troparion tones (used for the troparia and kontakia) have this particular voice setting. Here, we see that the *melody* is in the *soprano* part. The *melody harmonization*, again up parallel 3rd's from the melody itself, is in the *tenor* part. The *sustaining common tones* are here found in the *alto* part. And, once again, the *roots of the chords* are found in the *bass* part.

Again, the functionality of the parts determines the manner in which the hymn is sung. Therefore, since the sopranos have the melody here instead of the altos, the soprano part should be the loudest in volume. Next in both importance and volume should be the tenors, who have the melody harmonization. The basses, keeping their function of singing the roots of the chords, are again third in both importance and volume. Finally, with the singing of the sustaining common tones, the altos should be the softest in volume.

One final example should suffice for illustrating this concept of musical awareness. This is from the Georgian Chant setting of the Cherubic Hymn:

Example 8

all - earth ly cares, all - earth ly cares!

In this particular voice setting, the **melody** is in the **alto** part. However, unlike the other examples we have looked at, there is **no** melody harmonization up in parallel 3rd's. Rather, **all three other parts** (soprano, tenor, and bass) just fill in the chord tones (root, 3rd, 5th) of the harmonization of this setting. Therefore, the altos, having the one and only melody, should be the loudest part in volume, with all three other parts (soprano, tenor, and bass) singing **much** softer than the altos, in order to bring the melody part to the forefront.

The knowledge of the functionality of the various parts of the four sections of the choir for the choir singers, will ensure that the singing of our Orthodox hymnology will be done in a manner that is appropriate to this functionality.

5
REHEARSAL TECHNIQUES

There are three essential areas that need to be worked for proper singing by Church musicians: maintaining correct posture, the proper method of breathing, and tone placement. All of these elements are essential in order to sing in an appropriate manner to the glory of God.

A.   POSTURE

Correct posture and body alignment are crucial for quality singing. A person who exhibits poor posture, with their inner entrails misaligned and pressing together, cannot possibly manifest proper breath support and execute tones of quality and beauty. Good posture places the bodily organs in their appropriate position and ensures maximum strength and support for tone production of the highest order.

Concerning posture, the best and simplest concept to remember is "*back* and *down*": that is, the shoulders should be pulled back into a

comfortable position (not so far back that the
muscles are straining) and down, also to a point of
natural comfortability. A posture that is forward and
down leads to the round-shouldered position of bad
posture (like a person with osteoporosis), and a
posture that is back and up, with the shoulders
touching the ears, leads to a position of stiffness and
rigidity (like the Frankenstein monster in the
movies). A posture that keeps the shoulders back
and down, naturally and comfortably, ensures the
best positioning of the body. Along with this, singers
and choir directors may want to pursue ways to align
the body to its most natural and supportive
position.[15]

B.   BREATHING

The second essential element required for
quality singing is that of proper breathing and breath
support. Most people breathe in a shallow manner,
utilizing only their lungs. This may suffice for routine
activity and a sedentary lifestyle, but it is totally
inadequate for the task of choral music production.

---

[15] For a detailed presentation of proper body alignment, cf.
Evoking Sound, pp. 25-39.

The way to good breathing and breath support is to embrace your "DIB's": DIB, or Diaphragmatic Intercostal Breathing, is the practice of breathing throughout the entire cavity comprising the respiratory and digestive tracts. It consists of contracting the diaphragm, a muscle located horizontally between the chest cavity and the stomach cavity.[16]

The easiest way to learn and master the art of DIB is to either stand straight against a flat wall or, better yet, to lie down on your back on a floor or bed with firm back support. Placing your hand on your lower stomach area (right below the navel), take in a deep breath slowly while *simultaneously* pushing your hand out and up with your stomach. Think of it as similar to using a bellows for a fireplace or an accordion: as air enters, the bellows or accordion expands to let the maximum amount of air enter and fill up the unit. The same concept works with your body: as you breathe in while, at the same time, expanding your stomach up and out, you end up drawing air not only into your lungs but into your entire diaphragm and stomach cavity. Suddenly taking in this much higher quantity of air can initially result in lightheadedness, which is why it is recommended to begin this exercising lying down,

---

[16] Internet site, Wikipedia, under "Diaphragmatic Breathing."

rather than standing up. With regular and consisted practice, the body will naturally adjust to this new level of maximum air input, and the lightheadedness will quickly dissipate.

A healthy and humble way to begin is to lie down and practice this breathing for five minutes a day for the first week or two. During this time, just breathe deeply into your lower diaphragmatic area in a natural manner, neither forcing the air in or out, nor trying to hold your breath or the air in this lower cavity. After two or three weeks of practicing this, at which time the lightheadedness should dissipate, then, beginning with the fourth or fifth week, practice breathing naturally like this for five minutes, followed by five minutes of breathing in deeply, holding the breath in the lower diaphragmatic area for a few ***comfortable*** seconds, and then slowly releasing it. Again, a gradual buildup of this skill is essential. There is no need to try to become a "respiratory body-builder", and doing this exercise on a level of comfortability will ensure that no muscles are unnecessarily pulled or strained. After a week or two of this, continue the regular breathing cycle for the first five minutes and, in the second five minutes of holding the breath, try to increase the breath holding time by only a second or two. This is parallel to gradual bodybuilding: by increasing the held breath slowly and incrementally, you will consistently and *safely* build up the diaphragm muscles to a level of strength and support.

You will then discover it to be *much* easier to maintain a quality tone while singing, coupled with consistent pitch retention (many singers go "flat" in singing their notes because of improper breathing and poor breath support) and more successful sustained singing of longer notes in the hymns. This, in turn, leads to better phrasing in the liturgical singing (text phrases thereby don't end up chopped and fragmented), whereby the context of the liturgical hymns is better understood and more easily prayed with on the part of the congregation.

C. TONE PLACEMENT

Tone placement is literally what it sounds like: placing the tone in the head, the point of placement depending on the tone's pitch, volume, and length of sound. One way to think of the human body is to use the image of the "shepherd's hook": a side view of the body would show the nasal cavity, the roundness of the head, and then the vertical aspect of the rest of the body. This is illustrated below.

Example 9

Crown of head
↓

Nasal cavity ↓

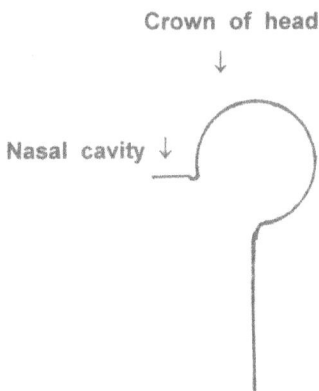

When a person sings a tone in the lower, more comfortable area of their pitch range (all the tones that they are able to sing, from lowest to highest), at a medium volume and for a short duration of time, that tone can be "placed" in the nasal cavity, in the middle area of the nose (considered vertically) and in front (considered horizontally). As this person sings up a scale or upwards in their pitch range, to higher tones, these subsequent tones need to be "placed" higher up in the nasal cavity, until, reaching the very highest tones in their range, the person would "place" the tone in the crown of the head. Likewise, for tones that require an increase in volume and/or duration, these tones would need to be "placed" higher in the nasal cavity, as well.

What does it mean, exactly, to "place" a tone? Simply put, it means projecting the tone to a specific place in the nasal cavity through imagining the tone already being in that specific place. So, for example, a woman singing soprano would sing a high-pitched tone by imagining that this tone is in the crown of her head. In other words, she would use her mind to project the tone upwards and "place" it in the crown of her head. The human mind and imagination are very powerful. Scientific studies have proven that people can, with training, actually control the functioning of their bodies through mental effort (regulating pulse and/or blood pressure, lowering body temperature, etc.). With regular, sustained, and patient practice, singers can gradually master the skill of placing tones at the various levels of the nasal and head cavities, based on the requirements of pitch, volume, and tone duration.[17] This skill,

---

[17] What I have referred to here as "tone placement" has been called "breath placement" or "air flow placement" by others who are expert at teaching proper singing techniques. Cf., especially, Holwey, Phil, *So You Want to Sing?*, Illustrations by Nancy Potts, Cover by Kathie Holwey, self-published by Philip L. Holwey, 1977, pp. 10-15 and 39-41 (available on Amazon.com). This is an *excellent* guide and textbook, fully

coupled with appropriate posture and
Diaphragmatic Intercostal Breathing and breath
support, will ensure the highest quality of tone
production and singing on the part of choir
members.

Proper rehearsal techniques are essential in
mastering the music to be sung at liturgical
services.[18]

D.   OPENING PRAYER

As previously stated, the **calling _from_ _God_** to
engage in liturgical singing is a **ministry**. As such, it is
more than appropriate for the choir director to
begin each rehearsal with an opening prayer. There
are many possibilities for such prayers to choose
from (such as the Lord's Prayer). One prayer that
has been found appropriate for the beginning of
choir rehearsals is the following:

---

illustrated, on the rudiments of posture, breathing, and tone
placement.

[18] The various topics discussed in this chapter are also
presented in expanded and detailed form in *Conducting*, pp.
121-216.

"O Christ our God, Who said, "Where two or three are gathered in My Name, there am I in the midst of them!", look down upon us now as we begin this choir rehearsal! Grant us to prayerfully master the music, with which we will worship You liturgically! May we perfect our singing in order to praise and glorify Your all – honorable and majestic Name: of the Father, and of the Son, and of the Holy Spirit, now and ever and unto ages of ages! Amen."

This prayer has a few key elements in it. First of all, it acknowledges the centrality of our Lord, Jesus Christ. Second, it quotes our Lord Himself directly from the Gospels. Third, it points seriously to the ministry of liturgical music and the need for prayerful preparation and mastery of the musical skills involved. Finally, it manifests the goal of all worship: the praise and glorification of the one God in the Holy Trinity: God the Father, the Son of God, and the Holy Spirit of God. A prayer such as this one, said by the choir director as he or she and all the singers bow their heads towards the holy sanctuary of the church, sets the correct spiritual tone and perspective for the serious work about to be done within the rehearsal.

E.   WARM – UP EXERCISES

After the opening prayer, it is best to begin the actual singing portion of the rehearsal with some vocal warm-up exercises. An appropriate start can be with exercises that teach and reinforce the basic concepts of posture, breathing, and tone placement. The following exercises can also be practiced by each Church singer personally at home.

One exercise that helps open up the throat and aids in good breath support is to sing the first five notes of a major scale up and then down, followed by a hold on the bottom note up a half-step. Then, using this raised half-step as the start of a new major scale, the singers would go up and down the first five notes of the new scale, ending on a hold on the bottom note of the new scale up a half-step again. This, in turn, begins the five-note process on a new scale. This can ascend until the singers are at the top of their *comfortable* range, that is, able to maintain good breath support and an open throat. They can then reverse the process by singing up and down the five notes of the major scale, ending on a hold a half-step below the ending note. A new scale then begins a half-step down, etc., until the bottom of the *comfortable* range for the singers is reached. Singing the notes on a ***non-solfege*** syllable (such as "doo") will free up the singers' concentration so they may focus on their proper singing techniques.

F.   DICTION EXERCISES

In order for the singing to be understood so that, as St Paul said, "I will sing with the spirit, and I will sing with the mind, also." (1 Cor 14:15), the words of the hymns must be pronounced clearly and intelligently. To accomplish this, it is helpful to spend some rehearsal time on diction exercises. One good source for those is the set of exercises by Liz T., found on the Internet at http://takelessons.com/blog/diction-exercises-z02. The following six exercises can prove to be most helpful in improving the diction of singers:

Tongue Twisters

Tongue twisters are good because they force a person to really focus on the pronunciation. A few helpful tongue twisters are:

- She sells seashells by the seashore.
- Red leather, yellow leather.
- Peter Piper picked a peck of pickled peppers.
- Who washed Washington's white woolen underwear, as Washington's washer woman went west?
- Mommy made me mash my M&M's.

Study Phonetics (IPA)

For this exercises, take a look at the song you're currently working on, and break down each word in the lyrics. Break apart the vowels, consonants, and diphthongs. Feel free to write in your score, if you need to spell a word differently for it to make sense in your singing.

Many singers refer to the IPA (International Phonetic Alphabet) when singing. This is a system derived from Latin that is used today as a standardized representation of sounds. It's a great tool for singers to use and study.

Practice Vowels

Take some time focusing on each of the vowels: *ah*, *ay*, *ee*, *oh*, and *oo*. Add a consonant at the beginning (such as "mah, may, me...") and sing through the list, making sure each one is clear.

Practice Consonants

Next, focus on consonants, like *D*, *T*, and *N*. Practice speaking the different sounds, repeating each a few times.

Lip Buzz and Trill

Warm up your lips, tongue, and teeth with simple lip buzzes and tongue trills.

Breath Support

Pick one of the tongue twisters above, and practice saying it all in one breath.

Again, improving diction makes the meaning of the hymns more intelligible, easier to understand, and more prayerful.

G.   PRE – SERVICE WARM – UP

Nowadays, many choirs gather together to do a warm-up immediately before a liturgical service. They will meet before a Vespers or a Divine Liturgy in a Church school classroom, the parish library, or in the large coffee hour room in the basement of the church building (if the choir meets for rehearsal on a Saturday afternoon before the Resurrectional Vespers, an added warm-up session is not necessary). This provides a double benefit for the singers: it gives them a chance to warm-up and stretch their vocal cords and breathing muscles before the service, and it also gives the choir director the opportunity to go over hymns that are specific to that particular liturgical service.

For example, if there is a given feast on a Sunday (say, Sunday of the Holy Cross during Great Lent, or Palm Sunday), the choir director will, at the pre-service warm-up, have the singers run through any special Antiphons, Troparia, Kontakia, special Trisagion, Prokeimena, Hymn to the Theotokos, and/or Communion Hymn that will be sung at that Divine Liturgy. Any musical trouble spots that were worked out at a previous rehearsal can be gone over again, to ensure that the singers have mastered the music at that point. Also, any places in the hymns where the wording of the liturgical text proved difficult can be sung through, to reinforce the clarity of the grammatical pronunciation on the part of the singers.

Usually, a pre-service warm-up is held a half-hour before the liturgical service begins. So, if the Sunday Divine Liturgy begins at 9 (or 9:30) am, the pre-service warm-up will commence at 8:30 (or 9) am, and conclude about ten to twelve minutes later. This gives the choir director a few minutes to go over the specifics to the reader who will be chanting the 3rd Hour that day, advising which troparia and

kontakia will be done at the specific points in the
Hour, which usually begins fifteen minutes before
the beginning of the Divine Liturgy. This also has the
added advantage of having all of the choir members
present to listen to the 3rd Hour, which will further
help them prepare themselves spiritually for singing
during the liturgical service.

H.   LITURGICAL AWARENESS
AND MUSICAL AWARENESS

Liturgical awareness refers to the function
that a hymn has within a liturgical service, a feast, or
an overall liturgical season. It therefore behooves
the choir director to become familiar with the
liturgical theology of the Orthodox Church, and there
are numerous books that cover this in detail.[19]

---

[19] Of particular importance and assistance are the works of Fr
Alexander Schmemann. Cf., for example, his *For the Life of
the World: Sacraments and Orthodoxy* (reprinted 2001), *Of
Water and the Spirit: A Liturgical Study of Baptism* (1974),
Great Lent: Journey to Pascha (revised edition 1974), and *The
Eucharist: Sacrament of the Kingdom* (1987), all SVS (St
Vladimir's Seminary) Press, Crestwood, NY.

Acquisition of this knowledge will enable the director to interpret the musical element of the hymns in the appropriate liturgical perspective, and also allow him or her to conduct the singing of this hymnology in a manner that reflects the reality of the particular service, feast, or liturgical season.

Musical awareness refers to the function of the musical elements within the hymnology of the liturgical services and their place and interaction within the various sections of the choir. Therefore, the choir members need to be musically proficient as to how the voicings in the different parts function and how to best reflect that function in the singing of the hymnology.

What does all this mean for the choir singers? The functionality of the parts determines which parts should be emphasized over others. Therefore, since the melody is in the alto part, the altos should be the most heard, that is, they should be the loudest part in volume, since, musically speaking, it is the most important part. Next in importance, with the melody harmonization up a 3rd, is the soprano part. This should be the next loudest part in volume. Third in importance, with the roots of the chords determining the musical harmonization, is the bass part. The basses, then, should sing more softly than

the altos and sopranos.   Here, in the final place of
importance with its use of the sustaining common
tones, is the tenor part, which should be the softest
in volume of the four parts. This does **not** mean that
the bass and tenor parts should not be heard, or that
the altos and sopranos should sing in an overly loud,
blasting manner. It **does** mean that the choir
director and all of the singers should be aware of the
musical function of all four parts, and adjust the
volume of each part accordingly to match and
manifest those functions. In fact, a good rule of
thumb for **all** singers should be this: If any singer
cannot hear the singers in the other three parts, that
singer is singing too loudly. So, even though the
altos here should sing louder than the other
sections, to bring out the main melody, they still
need to sing in such a manner that each alto can
hear the singing of the sopranos, the tenors, and the
basses. Singers in the other three sections should
sing accordingly, as well.

I.   INITIAL PREPARATION

Before singing any notes of a new
arrangement of a hymn, it is helpful to go over the

hymn from the viewpoints of liturgical awareness and musical awareness, as discussed in the previous chapter. So, for instance, looking at the Georgian Chant arrangement of the Cherubic Hymn that we looked at in chapter 8 (Example 84, pages 150-151), it is first suggested that the choir director discuss the place of the Cherubic Hymn in the Divine Liturgy, that it functions as the entrance hymn for the Eucharistic Entrance. Also worth mentioning is the fact that the two halves of the Cherubic Hymn are usually sung at a different tempo, the first half (through "all earthly cares") more slowly (to give the clergy time for their prayer, a small censing, the triple recitation of the Cherubic Hymn, and the preparation of the Holy Gifts on the Table of Oblation) and the second half (beginning with "Amen." and "That we may receive the King of all,…!") more briskly (since less time is required on the part of the clergy to place the Holy Gifts on the Altar Table, cense them, and then be ready to proceed with the following Litany of Supplication).

Another *very* good tool to use for liturgical awareness is, again before doing any singing, to read through the text of the hymn to be rehearsed. So many times, both choir directors and members sing the hymnology without paying any attention to the meaning of the text. In other words, they fail to **pray** with the hymns themselves. And, if the Church musicians sing without meaning, how can they hope to lead the rest of the congregation into praying with the hymnology?

It is after discussing these liturgical and musical elements with the choir members that the choir director can now turn to the actual singing of the hymn.

J.   FIRST RUN - THROUGH

The choir singers should begin by singing the melody part of the hymn (in his or her own comfortable range) all the way through, so they can hear the melody. Most choir members are not proficient at reading music and many do not read music at all, so that they tend to learn the music by rote. In singing this first run-through of the melody, it is advisable for the choir director to sing it at a slower pace than will actually be sung during the services. This gives the singers the chance to follow the music along on the page while simultaneously hearing the director sing their part. By going more slowly like this, the singers have a greater chance of hearing and remembering the notes and melody pattern so that, when they begin singing it for the first time, the possibility of them singing the right notes is maximized.

As mentioned, the choir director should sing the entire hymn all the way through the first time. Then, the director may, in singing it a second time, break the hymn down into smaller sections.

K.   FINE   TUNING

Once the various sections of the choir have pretty well mastered the notes in their respective parts of the hymn, you can concentrate on fine tuning the singing by concentrating on other elements. First of all, have your full choir sing together a few times, gradually building up the tempo from the slower, learning-the-notes pace to the actual tempo at which they will sing the hymn in the liturgical services.

Another important area to focus on is phrasing. Many choirs sing in a choppy manner, breathing in the middle of the line or textual phrase, thereby obscuring the meaning of the text. There are numerous settings of our hymnology in either fixed meter or in chant meter that still puts measure lines every so many notes along the way. Alert your singers to this situation, and make them aware to sing the hymn in complete thoughts and sentences. The previously-mentioned exercise of just speaking through the text, without music, is of great benefit here. If your singers are having a difficult time with the phrasing, go back to the speaking-the-text exercise and run through that a few times, having the choir members pay close attention to the textual phrasing.

Along with tempo and phrasing, careful time and attention will need to be given to balance and blend. The musical awareness on the part of the choir members will prove helpful here. Keeping the functionality of the various parts in mind will allow the singers to adjust their volume to provide the right balance to let the melodic lines sound forth. As previously mentioned, with this particular arrangement, the altos, having the one and only melody part, need to be heard above everyone else. The remaining three parts, filling in the chord notes and passing tones, need to sing much more softly. This is what is meant by the term "balance".

The term "blend" refers to the ability of all the choir members to sing in such a manner that it sounds like one voice doing the singing. Careful attention needs to be paid in rehearsals to ensure that the singers all come in together on the first note, end together on the cadence cut-off's, and blend together throughout the rest of the phrases. Here, again, the choir members need to listen to each other and to the other sections of the choir as they sing the hymns. Watching the choir director is imperative. If you find your singers are not watching well and have troubling blending, have them close their music binders and try singing portions of the hymns from memory, paying attention and watching the choir director intently so as to sing as one unit. Periodic reminders and closed-book practicing will result in better blending on the part of the singers.

L.   POSITIVE REINFORCEMENT

Two other elements are necessary for the successful mastery of music at the choir rehearsal. The first of these is positive reinforcement. As any teacher will tell you (and, in the context of the rehearsal, the choir director ***does*** function as a teacher), those who are learning, be they students in a school or singers in a choir, are still human beings with the accompanying frailties and emotions that we all have. As such, when trying to master new skills or acquire new knowledge, much hard work and effort is required to accomplish this task. This can prove to be very demanding, both physically and emotionally. Using positive reinforcement to encourage and guide your singers is absolutely essential. When working with a section on a difficult passage, as your singers gradually master the notes and expressive elements of the hymnology, all along the way the director should make short little comments, such as, "Good!", "Better!", "That's it!", "Now you've got it!", "Great!", etc. Along with helping to keep a casual, light, easy-going atmosphere to the rehearsal, positive reinforcement also serves as necessary feedback to let the choir members know when they are on the right track in learning the music.

Another element in keeping a light tone to the rehearsal is to use a sense of humor. Care needs to be taken to make sure that any humorous remarks are both appropriate and applicable to the situation. To cite an example, whenever the singers in my choir began to forget to use good posture and proper breath support, resulting in a flattening of the notes of the hymn, I would remind them that, if they watched me, the director, intently, they would see that I was standing with good posture and was also periodically gesturing towards my abdomen to remind them of proper breath support. Watching me in that manner would therefore help them to stand properly, breathe correctly, and keep the pitch up. I would then end this explanation by saying, "In other words, if you see sharp ($C^{\#}$), you won't be flat (B^{b})!" This would be followed by some light laughter on the part of the singers. Yet, using humor in this manner of it being a teaching tool is very effective. The choir members, in remembering the humorous phrase, would tend to retain for a longer time the awareness of the need for good posture and proper breath support. Again, this element needs to be used sparingly, in order for the rehearsal not to devolve into a stand-up act in a comedy club. However, periodic use of humor as a teaching tool for difficult musical passages can prove to be very helpful.

M.   PHRASING

Another ***very*** important aspect of Orthodox liturgical singing that needs to be extensively dealt with in rehearsals is the concept of phrasing. What is absolutely ***essential*** in the celebration of our services is that the content of the hymnody, the text, is ***prayerfully intelligible***. That is, the meaning of the text needs to make sense so that the people may interiorize it and liturgically celebrate it in a prayerful manner. Alas, too often this is the liturgical component that is overlooked and slips through the cracks, so to speak. Consider, for example, the singing of "Lord, I Call Upon You" at Vesoers. In this hymn, for example, the singers would, with***out*** conscious focus and rehearsal on the part of the choir director, tend to take a breath or a break after the word "prayer," which is on a half note. This would result in the fragmenting of the meaning of the text. While it is true that the first part of this phrase, "Receive the voice of my prayer," could stand independently on its own, the same can***not*** be said of the second part of the phrase, "when I call upon You." This, in and by itself, is an ***in***complete thought, leading one to ask the question, "***What about*** 'when I call upon You'?" The answer is found in the ***complete*** phrase, "***Receive the voice of my prayer*** when I call upon You!"

This is a ***vital*** and ***essential*** element of our liturgical singing. It is imperative that all choir directors become acutely aware of the content of ***complete*** phrases in our hymnology, and accordingly rehearse the singers to sing that hymnology in ***complete*** thoughts and sentences.

N.   WOODSHEDDING

The term "woodshedding" refers to the practice of breaking down difficult musical passages into workable units of notes so that each unit of only a few notes can be focused on and mastered. As a person may take a piece of wood and, using a knife, whittle away at the wood until it is shaped into an object (a flute, a pen, etc.), so the singers focus on these small units of notes in order to "whittle" away the difficulty in mastering these notes. Then, as each group is mastered, it is then paired again with the other units of notes around it until the musical phrase is sung successfully in its entirety. The essence of woodshedding is to break problematic

areas down to the isolated notes in question,
rehearsing them correctly quite a few times to
master the particular musical problem in the small
unit, and then to regroup the small unit back to the
larger phrase unit once again.

O.   ATTENDING REHEARSALS

All of what has been presented above can only be
effective, naturally, if choir members come to
rehearsals. It can be very frustrating for the choir
director and the few people who *do* show up when
the majority of the group is absent. Not only that,
but it is also patently unfair to the conscientous
singers who *are* at the rehearsals to work diligently
to master the music, only to have those who are
absent come to the services, not having rehearsed
the specifics of the music involved, and then sing in a
manner that undoes all that was accomplished at the
rehearsal. There are various ways to handle this,
and each parish choir has its own policy regarding
rehearsal attendance. Some have a hard-and-fast
rule that says if a singer misses, say, three rehearsals

in a row, they must refrain from singing in the choir at services until they can regularly attend again. Other parishes have no policy at all, or they choose not to deal with the situation. Still others have established a policy that comes somewhere in between the two outlined above. Whatever policy is established, it is important that it be carried out consistently with *every* member of the choir, not playing favorites and having a double standard for privileged people. It is also very important that, whenever having to speak to a lapsed singer, that it be done privately to avoid embarrassment, and also that it be done in a firm but loving manner. It behooves the choir director to master the techniques outlined in this chapter, so that the rehearsals are productive and positively encouraging, so that singers will have the self-motivation to look forward to and *want* to attend rehearsals.

P.   TEXTUAL STUDY
AND MEDITATION

Another element of preparation can be discussed here. It would prove very beneficial for the choir director to provide copies of the texts for major feasts of the Church to his or her singers. The texts for Vespers and the Divine Liturgy may be found in their respective service books. These service books also include the texts from the Oktoechos, the Eight Tones, which change for the "Lord, I Call" and Aposrikha verses at Vespers and the Troparion, Kontakion, Prokeimenon, and "Alleluia" Verses at the Divine Liturgy. Photocopying the pages with the texts for, say, as a beginning, the Twelve Major Feasts, and then distributing them to the singers in the choir will provide an opportunity for these singers to study the texts of the festal hymnography and then meditate on them.

The importance of this is revealed in Scripture by a text from St Paul. In 1 Corinthians 14:15, he says, "I will pray with the spirit, and I will pray with the mind, also! I will sing with the spirit, and I will sing with the mind, also!" This text, with the two parallel, almost identical sentences, manifests the direct connect and link between prayer and liturgical singing. What we can see from this connection is this: If the choir singers study and understand the texts, and then meditate deeply on their meaning, this understanding and assimilation of the meaning of the text will come out in the way the choir members sing the hymns. They will truly be "sing(ing) with the spirit, and...sing(ing) with the mind, also!" In turn, the rest of the faithful in the congregation who are listening to these hymns will be able to "receive" more deeply the meaning of the hymns and pray along with them in the liturgical worship. The slight cost of photocopying and then studying these texts will pay off handsomely in spiritual dividends within the parish community.

Q.   MUSICAL TRAINING

One final element of preparation to be discussed is that of musical training. While it is true that the majority of choir singers over the centuries could not read music but learned the melodic lines of the hymns by rote, nevertheless, in our modern

times, it would behoove any choir member who
takes their ministry of singing seriously to consider
attending a night class in basic music reading.
Learning the elementary fundamentals of the names
of the lines and spaces on both staves (the treble
staff *and* the bass staff), along with the key
signatures of the major and minor keys up to and
including three sharps or flats, would give such a
singer a tremendous advantage in mastering the
music at rehearsals much quicker and more
efficiently. Another possibility is taking an evening
course in sight singing. Mastering the syllables of
the Movable Do System and applying it in learning
new musical settings within the context of a sight
singing class would immeasurably improve the choir
member's learning ability to master new musical
settings of our Orthodox liturgical hymnography.

6
LITURGICAL TEAMWORK

One final subject that needs to be addressed in regards to the ministry of Orthodox liturgical music is the extremely vital relationship between the choir director and singers and the main celebrant of the liturgical services. Though, at times, this may be the diocesan bishop or the Metropolitan (usually during a pastoral visit, the dedication of a church building, or a significant parish anniversary), most of the time this refers to the priest who is the pastor of that particular parish (the other exception may be a priest who is filling in for the pastor who is away on vacation or ill). Since the liturgical singing comprises an average of 75% of the services (more during the Pascha season, less during Great Lent), the coordination and cooperation between these two people has great influence and lasting repercussions on the life of the parish community.

A.   "... DECENTLY AND IN ORDER!"

The foundational basis for the relationship between the choir director and the main celebrant is given to us scripturally by St Paul:

"But, all things should be done decently and in order!" (1 Corinthians 14:40).

Here, we have the fundamental reference for *all* ministries within the Church: everything, whether it be celebrating the liturgical services, education, mission, outreach, giving alms, or whatever, needs to be done in a manner that reflects the peace of Christ (Who *is* our Peace!) and the "righteousness and peace and joy in the Holy Spirit!" (Romans 14:17). This is further reflected in the fruit of the Holy Spirit, as enumerated by St Paul:

"But, the fruit of the Spirit is love, joy, peace, patience, kindness, goodness, faithfulness, gentleness, self-control!" (Galatians 5:22).

With this as the "canon", the measuring stick and reference point, both the choir director and the main celebrant can work together in a loving and harmonious manner, to work out the details of the liturgical services so that the flow of these very services goes along smoothly and efficiently.

B. THE MAIN CELEBRANT AS THE REFERENCE POINT

With this in mind, even though it is not an official canon of the Orthodox Church, it has been the practice within the Holy Tradition down through the centuries that the main celebrant is the reference point for all decisions and details concerning the celebration of the liturgical services. Again, most of the time, this main celebrant will be the priest who is the pastor of the local parish. However, if the diocesan bishop is presiding, he, then, becomes the main celebrant and makes the final decisions regarding liturgical details. If, furthermore, the Metropolitan is present to preside, then he supercedes the authority of both the parish priest and the diocesan bishop. Thus, by acknowledging and respecting each person in his or her position of function of ministry within the Church, the celebration of the liturgical services done in a manner "decently and in order" is ensured. Everyone needs to embrace the humility to acquiesce to the next person in the hierarchy of ministries. This applies as equally to the parish priest (when the diocesan bishop is present) and to the diocesan bishop (when the Metropolitan is present) as it does to the choir director.

C.   THE LITURGICAL BLESSING

As an acknowledgement of this reality of the main celebrant as the liturgical reference point, it has started becoming the practice in some parishes for the choir director, before the liturgical service begins, to approach the main celebrant and receive a liturgical blessing to direct the choir and (by extension) the entire liturgical community in the musical responses. This is a good practice that, hopefully, will extend to more and more parishes. The reason for such is the following: All of the liturgical celebrants within the sanctuary, whether they be the deacon(s), the altar servers, the priest(s) (if there be a bishop or Metropolitan presiding), need to approach the main celebrant for a blessing to serve in the sanctuary. Throughout the service itself, a deacon (if there be any serving) will, at different times, bow to the priest as he goes to exit the sanctuary to chant the next litany. If there is a bishop or Metropolitan presiding, any of the priests serving will bow and receive a blessing from the

bishop to chant the following prayer or exclamation.
If, then, it is important for these celebrants to
manifest the humility and obedience due to the
main celebrant throughout the services, is it not
important, also, for the choir director, who (as we
have stated) will be directing about 75% of the
liturgical activity, to also manifest his or her humility
and obedience by asking for a similar blessing from
the main celebrant? This brings about positive
results on a couple of levels. First of all, it is a daily
reminder to the choir director, when he or she
receives the liturgical blessing, to work together with
the main celebrant in humility and obedience, so
that the services flow smoothly with all those
actively involved in celebrating the services knowing
what will occur and everyone being, so to speak, "on
the same page". Secondly, there are some clergy
(priests and bishops) who, not having musical
knowledge or proficiency, feel uncomfortable or
distrustful when relating with the choir director. By
submitting himself or herself in humility and
obedience to the main celebrant through the
receiving of the liturgical blessing, the priest or
bishop is quite often put at ease, knowing that the
choir director will cooperatively work with him to
ensure that the coordination of the liturgical details
will be carried out appropriately. Anything that can

be done to enhance mutual trust is to be embraced, and the giving of the liturgical blessing can go a long way to building that trust.

Besides the choir director, if other choir members wish to receive a blessing from the main celebrant, I am sure if they ask their parish priest, he would be more than happy to accommodate them, knowing full well that these Church singers are taking their ministry in the choir very seriously.

D.   CONSTRUCTIVE COMMUNICATION

Establishing humility, obedience, and a bond of trust through the practice of giving the liturgical blessing, the main celebrant and the choir director now need to work out the details and liturgical specifics of the services through the use of an open and constructive communication. Again, with some priests and bishops feeling "out of their element" because of a lack of musical proficiency, they may seem initially uncomfortable discussing liturgical details with someone who is very much at home with both the liturgical services and the musical hymnology with which those services are celebrated. Here, the choir director needs to practice some pastoral compassion and patience, gently working and communicating openly with the celebrant to ensure that the director's expertise in musical matters does not appear overwhelming or liturgically threatening to the celebrant. By communicating in a manner that is open, gentle, honest, above-board, and informed (both the choir director and the main celebrant are well-trained and versed in the specifics of the services), the director can show the celebrant that having knowledge does not necessarily mean having control, domination, or power, but means that both persons can intelligently and efficiently work out the details and directives of the services so that the various ministries of the services are celebrated cooperatively and in unity.

This system of open communication, however, needs to be a two-way endeavor. If the main celebrant is the person who is to determine the liturgical specifics of a given service, then he needs to be open, honest, and clear about those specifics and communicate these directives to the choir director. To make a sudden change in a service while failing to communicate this change to the director and then expect him or her to assume what is going to happen or to somehow read the mind of the main celebrant is patently unfair. It takes very little effort to explain and instruct a director on any liturgical changes or differences that will occur that day. If, for instance, a set of icons is to be prayed over and blessed near the end of the Divine Liturgy, the celebrant needs to inform the director of this added event, specifically outlining that the people will sing "Blessed be the Name of the Lord" twice, then the prayers and blessing of the icons will take place with the appropriate responses, and then, finally, as the clergy reenter the sanctuary, the people will sing the third and final rendition of "Blessed be the Name of the Lord". There are times when such events come about last-minute, so to speak, as with the blessing of specific items such as icons. However, most special events are known well in advance, such as receiving new catechumens into the parish community (whereby a specific prayer is chanted and responded to at the beginning of the Litany of the Catechumens) or celebrating a baptismal or matrimonial Divine Liturgy. Since these circumstances are known weeks or even months before the events take place, it is fitting and appropriate for the celebrant to advise the choir director of the event ***well in advance***, and to give sufficient allotted time to go over the specifics of the service with the director, as well as giving the director ample time to organize the musical elements of the event and successfully prepare his or her choir with plenty of rehearsal time available. If the celebrant fails to do this and things do not go well with the special liturgical event, then the celebrant has no one to blame for this but himself. Well-planned advisement, communication, and directives, however, will maximize the possibility that the celebration of the special liturgical event will go smoothly, peacefully, and joyfully.

Such open communication can immensely help build a rapport and a relationship of trust and mutual respect that can be both beneficial to the parish community and enjoyable to both the choir director and the main celebrant for years to come.

E.   THE EXPERTISE OF THE CHOIR DIRECTOR

One final word needs to be said, this time from the perspective of the choir director. While the director needs to be humble, obedient, and cooperative in regards to the authority of the main celebrant for the decisions of celebrating the liturgical services, the main celebrant needs to be mindful and respectful, as well, of the expertise of the choir director. Many people, even Church singers and choir members, have no concept of the long training, preparation, and practice of skills that is needed to be an effective and proficient choir director. Especially when a director has a very relaxed and smooth directing style, many people come to the erroneous conclusion that this ministry is exceedingly simple, needs hardly any training, and that just about anyone who can carry a tune can easily get up in front of the singers and direct the liturgical hymnology. Nothing could be further from the truth! As the information and examples presented in this book show, it takes a *lot* of time, effort, and slow, patient hard work to master the various skills necessary to become a worthy minister of Orthodox liturgical music. While being the person who specifically makes Christ present in the parish community and has the prerogative of making the final decisions regarding the services, the main celebrant also needs to acknowledge the training and expertise, musical, liturgical, and otherwise, of the choir director, and be open to constructive feedback and suggestions regarding the celebration of the liturgical services. Again, with both parties living a life of prayer, repentance, and humility, an open, loving, and constructively working relationship can be established and deepened between the main celebrant and the choir director, so that the specifics of the liturgical services may be worked out peacefully and efficiently, in order for these services to be celebrated "decently and in order".

7
LIVING OUT THE GOSPEL

A. CHOIR DIRECTOR AS MUSICAL "PASTOR"

In some ways, the choir director acts as a musical "pastor" to his or her singers in the choir. Certain aspects of the choir director's ministry parallel that of the parish priest. First of all, the choir director is a **leader**. He or she is in a position of authority, leadership, and respect. Therefore, just as with the parish priest, the choir director needs to set an example in his or her behavior, modeling the Christian virtues in his or her daily life. The parish priest needs to comport himself in a way that leads his flock to imitate the Christian virtues he manifests, and the same is true of the leadership role of the choir director.

Second, as with the parish priest, the choir director has, in the directing ministry, the characteristic of being a **guide** to the singers. The parish priest guides his flock through preaching, teaching, the Sacrament of Confession, spiritual counseling, etc. The choir director guides the singers through the teaching aspect of the choir rehearsal.

This is true not just of the musical elements themselves, but, also, of the dogmatic teachings of the Church that are manifested in the texts of the hymns and the various feasts celebrated throughout the liturgical year. Engaging in this doctrinal teaching is just as important an example of spiritual guidance as a counseling session is with the parish priest. Both are ways that the Orthodox Christian singer deepens his or her understanding of the Faith and, in turn, moves forward in spiritual growth.

Third, the choir director, along with the parish priest, has to practice the element of ***pastoral discernment*** in his or her ministry. There may be times when a singer cannot fulfill their musical commitment of their choir ministry. This may be for various reasons, depending on what is currently going on in the life of that particular choir member. The choir director may need to speak privately with the concerned singer in order to learn what is happening. Depending on circumstances, the choir director may just need to listen to the person share their concerns, or he or she may need to advise the singer to take a sabbatical from the choir until the specific situation is resolved. Even at other times, with less critical situations, the choir director may notice one of the singers not feeling well, or seeming to be upset or depressed. Just as the parish priest, in his pastoral ministry, may need to take a few minutes to show concern for a member of his flock, so, too, the choir director, sensing something amiss with one of the singers, may need to spend a few minutes showing concern and giving comfort to the specific singer.

Finally, as with the parish priest, the choir director needs to be able to juggle the needs of many people within a single group. In other words, there needs to be a ***community-level pastorship***, so to speak, that the director needs to deal with. The parish priest needs to be able to handle conflicting situations between members of the one parish community in a way that addresses the needs of both parties. The choir director, also, may find, at times, that he or she needs to sensitively deal with conflicting situations between various singers in the choir, or, even, between various sections of the choir, such as between sopranos and altos, or between tenors and basses. Having the necessary skills to minister to various people with different needs and levels of spiritual grown is as essential for the choir director as it is for the parish priest.

B.   "WORKING OUT YOUR
OWN SALVATION"

In the section of the previous chapter dealing with textual study and meditation, we quoted the phrase from St Paul in 1 Corinthians, where he said, "I will pray with the spirit, and I will pray with the mind, also! I will sing with the spirit, and I will sing with the mind, also!" (1 Cor 14:15). Again, as we stated at that time, there is a direct connection and link between prayer and liturgical singing. Taking this a step further, we can say that, since prayer deals with connecting with God in the heart, the spiritual state of a person's heart and, therefore, of their life of repentance, will *also* have a direct connection between this state of the heart and liturgical singing. This is *not* a far-fetched idea. Many, if not most, of us Orthodox have, at some point in our lives, visited other Orthodox parishes, whether while on vacation, visiting family in other cities, or even, if we have moved into a new area, checking out local parishes. It is also proper to assume that most of us who *have* done such parish visiting have been exposed to many different types of parish communities. Some of them are made up of warm, loving people who take seriously the Gospel, have the love of God and neighbor in their hearts, believe in the missionary ministry of the Church, etc. Other parishes, however, are unfortunately made up of people who have an agenda radically opposed to the Gospel. They may be hanging on to a certain ethnic heritage, or are content with maintaining their self-enclosed group of "acceptable" people, who are very cold and hard towards visitors, and who have long ago driven their children and grandchildren away from the Church because these young people failed to see even a tiny hint of the love of God in these communities. I, myself, have experienced both types of parish communities, and it is on this basis that I propose the following questions: Did you not notice, in the cold, self-enclosed parishes, a certain emptiness in the way the hymns of the liturgical services were sung? Did not the singing prove to be totally lacking in the invisible, yet so obviously detectable, qualities of the love, joy, and peace of God that should be radiating from the choir and others who join in the singing? Furthermore, did not the singing reflect the cold, sterile social atmosphere of such a parish community? Did not the singing and the social and spiritual atmosphere of such a community remind you of what the Lord once said? He states in St

Matthew's Gospel, "Woe to you, scribes and Pharisees, hypocrites! For, you are like whitewashed tombs, which outwardly appear beautiful, but within they are full of dead men's bones and all uncleanness! So, you, also, outwardly appear righteous to men, but within you are full of hypocrisy and iniquity!" (Matthew 23:27-28).

Now, turn your memory back to a visit of the aforementioned type of parish community, the ones where the warmth, kindness, and inviting spirit of the people of this particular parish reflected that love, joy, and peace of God that is so present in such a parish. When visiting such a community, did you not notice, in a very real, obvious, concrete, and tangible way, that the singing of the liturgical hymns lifted you up? Did not the singing reflect that warmth, kindness, invitation, love, joy, and peace of God that so obviously lives and breathes in such a community? And, in listening to and worshipping with such liturgical singing, did it not lift up your spirit to the point where, along with the emissaries of St Vladimir who returned to him from their trip to Constantinople, you could say that you didn't know if you were in Heaven or on Earth? It should be clear, from these two examples, that the ***inner*** state of the singers is reflected in the ***outer*** activity of their liturgical singing, and that the example of the warm, loving parish community is the one that we should aspire to.

Why was this *presence* of God so clearly manifested in such a warm, loving community? Because, the people there *invited* God into their community. They invited Him into their *community* because each parishioner *personally invited Him into their hearts!* Each member of that Gospel-centered community took seriously St Paul's words, when he admonished each and every one of us to "work out your own salvation with fear and trembling!" (Philippians 2:12).

Therefore, it behooves each and every Orthodox Christian to do precisely that, to work out his or her own salvation in fear and trembling. And, if this is important for the general parishioner, isn't it even more critical for the Church musician, who has accepted the ministry of singing the liturgical hymns that comprise, on the average, 75% of our liturgical services, to do so even more? Along with all that has been presented previously in this book, from liturgical and spiritual preparation, to understanding the iconographical aspects of liturgical music, to learning and mastering the various musical and rehearsal skills presented, should not the liturgical musician, as part of their *liturgical* and *spiritual*

ministry, strive to internalize the contents of the liturgical services, from the prayers to the hymns to the Scriptural readings, to make them their own?

8
FELLOWSHIP OF ORTHODOX LITURGICAL MUSICIANS

A.   SHARING THE MINISTRY

   While it is preferable that parish communities do not devolve into collectives of individual organizations, still, there *is* a special relationship that develops between Orthodox choir singers that results from working together in rehearsals and singing the responses during the liturgical services. This is because all of these people together are sharing the ministry of Orthodox liturgical singing, a ministry that has a special place all its own within each parish community. This common working together (and, the word "liturgy" literally means "common work" or "common action"), with long hours struggling to learn new music, refine the liturgical singing, and sharing the teachings of the Church that are inherent in the liturgical hymns, forms a special bond between those people engaged in this glorious ministry. Within the family of the parish community, then, the choir and its members seem to constitute a "family within the family."

B.   SPECIAL FELLOWSHIP
IN SPECIAL REHEARSALS

Sharing this ministry together, there are ways that Orthodox liturgical choir members can share even more special fellowship with one another. One possibility is in the form of special rehearsals. There are times during the liturgical year, especially during Great Lent and Holy Week, when small groups or ensembles come together to sing portions of the services. Examples of this include trios for "Let My Prayer Arise" for the Liturgy of the Presanctified Gifts, a small ensemble for the "Hymn of Cassia" at the Matins of Holy Wednesday, other small combinations of singers for "The Wise Thief" at the Matins of Holy Friday, and a quartet or quintet for the Exapostilarion at Paschal Matins. All of these situations, plus other combinations of singers (such as trios, quartets, men's choir, and women's choir), provide opportunities for these small ensembles to come together.

These small ensembles, therefore, need to rehearse the specifics of the special hymn or hymns that they will be singing. One possibility or opportunity is for these small ensembles to gather together at the home of one of the singers on a weeknight or a weekend. Each member of the small ensemble can bring a dish to share at a collective potluck supper that can follow the rehearsal (it is best *not* to do the singing on a full stomach). Getting together for a small rehearsal followed by a simple meal like this can make what can seem to be a drudgery of hard work be more of an enjoyable experience to look forward to. This can even be done during Great Lent (it is best *not* to have any rehearsals during Holy Week). Special ensembles or collectives of choir singers can plan a weeknight rehearsal during Great Lent that can be followed with a Lenten-type simple meal afterwards. Great Lent *is* a time of fasting and repentance, but it does *not* have to be a time where we shun our relationships with our Christian brothers and sisters.

C.   SPECIAL FELLOWSHIP IN SPECIAL EVENTS

Again, while a parish should not become a collective of separated organizations, still, there is a special bond shared by those who calling are to partake of the joyful ministry of Orthodox liturgical singing. This bond is especially strong between the members of the parish choir, who work so hard together throughout the liturgical year through their sharing choir rehearsals, special small groups such as trios, quartets, and octets, and singing the various hymns at the regular services of the Church year, as well as special feasts and seasons, such as Great Lent and Holy Week. Many times, this important ministry is overlooked or taken for granted by the parish at large. A couple of things can be suggested to increase the fellowship and appreciation of this musical ministry.

First of all, the parish can set aside a certain time to recognize and thank the choir director and choir members for the hard work undertaken during the liturgical year. Since October 1st commemorates *two* liturgical musicians, St Romanus the Melodist and St John Koukouzelis the Hymnographer, the first Sunday of October would be a natural occasion each year for the parish community to show their appreciation and recognition for this work. This can be as simple as mentioning all of this during the announcements at the end of the Divine Liturgy, and including the choir director and choir members among the people mentioned for singing "Many Years!" after the conclusion of the announcements. Some parishes may wish to get a cake from a local bakery to serve at the Coffee Hour, with the simple inscription, "Thank you, Choir!" placed on the cake.

The choir members themselves can also organize special social events throughout the year. Having a choir dinner during the festive seasons following Pascha and Christmas would be an appropriate way for the singers to share in joyful celebration. A choir picnic sometime during the summer months can also provide an opportunity to share food and fellowship during the season when parents and children have a break from the rigors of the school year.

Parish priests, choir directors, and choir members may come up with other ways of sharing fellowship at special choir events. Using one's imagination to think of creative avenues for such fellowship reaps great rewards during the liturgical year, and brings the joy of God and the Church to this most special of Church ministries!

BIBLIOGRAPHY

Music

Christ, William; DeLone, Richard; Kliewer, Vernon; Rowell, Lewis; and Thomson, William; *Materials and Structure of Music, Volume 1*, 2nd Edition, Prentice Hall, Englewood Cliffs, New Jersey, 1972. Introductory material presented on a college freshman language level.

Jones, George Thaddeus, *Music Theory*, Barnes and Noble (Harper and Row), New York, New York, 1974. Easier reading than *Materials*, but not as complete.

Lamb, Gordon H., *Choral Techniques*, William C. Brown Company, Dubuque, Iowa, 1976. Written for teaching singing in schools, it is nevertheless helpful, especially in the area of rehearsal technique.

Rudolf, Max, The *Grammar of Conducting*, 2nd Edition, Schirmer Books, Macmillan Publishing Company, Inc., New York, New York, 1980. The most complete conducting book written, both for choral and instrumental music.

Liturgical Music

von Gardner, Johann, **Russian Church Singing, Volume 1: Orthodox Worship and Hymnography**, St Vladimir's Seminary (SVS) Press, Crestwood, New York, 1980. A must for all liturgical musicians, it presents the structure and rubrics of the services of the Orthodox Church, as well as examining the essence of liturgical music.

Wellecz, Egon, **A History of Byzantine Music and Hymnography**, 2nd Edition, Oxford at the Clarendon Press, Oxford, England, 1980. The authoritative work on Byzantine chant.

Douglas, Winfred, **Church Music in History and Practice**, Charles Scribner's Sons, New York, New York, 1937. Written by a Protestant, it is a valuable book on liturgical singing, particularly in the relationship of music and text.

Theology

Hopko, Father Thomas, **The Orthodox Faith: An Elementary Handbook on the Orthodox Church**, Department of Religious Education, Orthodox Church in America, New York, New York, 1971. Written in four volumes (*I: Doctrine*; *II: Worship*; *III: Bible and Church History*; *IV: Spirituality*), this series presents the teachings of the Orthodox Faith in a clear, easy-to-read format that is very understandable. Illustrated.

Schmemann, Alexander, *Introduction to Liturgical Theology*, SVS Press, Crestwood, New York, 1986. A deep book that should be re-read many times, it is, however, invaluable for a correct perspective of the liturgical situation in the Orthodox Church.

Ware, Archimandrite Kallistos (Timothy), *The Orthodox Church*, Penguin Books, New York, New York, 1963. A thorough handbook of the Orthodox Church, it discusses its history, faith, and worship.

Music Books

Drillock, David; Erickson, John H.; and Erickson, Helen Breslich, eds.; *The Divine Liturgy*, SVS Press, Crestwood, New York, 1982. Contains settings of hymns for the Liturgy from various traditions. Also by SVS Press are: *Holy Week: Volumes 1, 2, and 3*; *Pascha: The Resurrection of Christ*; and *The Liturgy of the Presanctified Gifts*.

Liturgical Books

Hapgood, Isabel Florence, ***Service Book of the Holy Orthodox-Catholic Apostolic Church***, 4th Edition, Syrian Antiochian Orthodox Archdiocese, Brooklyn, New York, 1965. Although the translations are quite archaic, the book does present all the services of the Church.

Nassar, the late Reverend Seraphim, ***Divine Prayers and Services of the Catholic Orthodox Church of Christ***, Antiochian Orthodox Christian Archdiocese, Englewood, New Jersey, 1979. Also archaic in textual usage, it nevertheless presents the rubrical propers of the liturgical services.
Ware, Archimandrite Kallistos and Mother Mary; ***The Festal Menaion***, Faber and Faber, London, England, 1969. Texts of the Twelve Major Feasts.

_____; ***The Lenten Triodion***, Faber and Faber, London, England, 1978. Texts of Great Lent, from the Sunday of the Publican and the Pharisee to Holy Saturday.

Liturgical Theology

Schmemann, Alexander, *For the Life of the World: Sacraments and Orthodoxy* (reprinted 2001), SVS Press, Crestwood, NY.

_____ , *Of Water and the Spirit: A Liturgical Study of Baptism* (1974), SVS Press, Crestwood, NY.

_____ , *Great Lent: Journey to Pascha* (revised edition 1974), SVS Press, Crestwood, NY.

_____ , *The Eucharist: Sacrament of the Kingdom* (1987), SVS Press, Crestwood, NY.

www.ingramcontent.com/pod-product-compliance
Lightning Source LLC
Chambersburg PA
CBHW071230090426

42736CB00014B/3027